Scholastic BookFiles™

A READING GUIDE TO

Shiloh

by Phyllis Reynolds Naylor

Jeannette Sanderson

SCHOLASTIC REFERENCE

W9-CDI-103

Library of Congress Cataloging-in-Publication Data
Sanderson, Jeannette.
Scholastic BookFiles: A Reading Guide to Shiloh by
Phyllis Reynolds Naylor / Jeannette Sanderson.
p. cm.
Summary: Discusses the writing, characters, plot, and themes of this 1992 Newbery Award–winning book. Includes discussion questions and activities.
Includes bibliographical references (p.).
1. Naylor, Phyllis Reynolds. Shiloh—Juvenile literature.
2. Human–animal relationships in literature—Juvenile literature.
3. West Virginia—In literature—Juvenile literature. 4. Dogs in literature—Juvenile literature. [1. Naylor, Phyllis Reynolds. Shiloh.
2. American literature—History and criticism.] I. Title: A Reading Guide to Shiloh by Phyllis Reynolds Naylor. II. Title.
PS3564.A9 S4837 2003
813′.54—dc21   2002191230
0-439-46329-7
10 9 8 7 6 5 4 3 2 1   03 04 05 06 07
Composition by Brad Walrod/High Text Graphics, Inc.
Cover and interior design by Red Herring Design
Printed in the U.S.A.   23
First printing, July 2003

Contents

"I'm not happy unless I spend some time, every day, writing."

—Phyllis Reynolds Naylor

Phyllis Reynolds Naylor loves to write. And she writes a lot. She has written more than one hundred books and more than two thousand short stories and articles. She writes for children, teenagers, and adults. How can anyone write so much? Was she born writing? Well, just about.

Phyllis Dean Reynolds was born on January 4, 1933, in Anderson, Indiana. She was the second of three children, with an older sister and a younger brother. Her mother was a homemaker, and her father was a salesman. It was the Great Depression, and the family moved around a lot in search of hard-to-find jobs for Mr. Reynolds.

While the family's hometown changed often, their nighttime ritual did not. Eugene or Lura Mae Reynolds read to their three children every night. This planted the seed for their middle child to become a writer. "I loved stories as far back as I can remember," Naylor says, "because my parents read aloud to us every night."

Naylor began writing her very own books in fourth grade. She remembers: "Each day I would rush home from school to see if the wastebasket held any discarded paper that had one side blank. We were not allowed to use new sheets of paper for our writing and drawing, so books had to be done on used paper. I would staple these sheets together and sometimes paste a strip of colored paper over the staples to give it the appearance of a bound book. Then I would grandly begin my story, writing the words at the top of each page and drawing an accompanying picture on the bottom. And sometimes I even cut old envelopes in half and pasted them on the inside covers as pockets, slipping an index card in each one, like a library book, so I could check it out to friends and neighbors. I was the author, illustrator, printer, binder, and librarian, all in one."

Naylor wrote hundreds of these books. The young author's creativity wasn't limited to books, however. "I always loved to make things," she says. "If I wasn't writing I would be making pot holders or building things out of wood. I loved to have a finished product in my hand."

When Naylor was sixteen, her first story was published in a church magazine. As much as she loved to write, however, she didn't begin her career as a writer right away. "I did not know that writing would be my life's work until I was in my late twenties," she says. She had been writing all that time, and submitting stories to small magazines, but writing wasn't her full-time job. She worked as a teacher, a locker-room attendant, a secretary, and an editorial assistant before she dedicated herself completely to writing.

Naylor began her writing career in 1960. Five years later, her first book—the short story collection *The Galloping Goat and Other Stories*—was published. Her first novel, *What the Gulls Were Singing*, was published two years later. Naylor has published at least one book a year ever since.

The author credits her success to her persistence. "If I hadn't stuck with it, if I hadn't tried to make my next story better than the one before, I probably wouldn't ever have gotten up the courage to write books," she says. Where did she learn never to give up? From her father. Naylor says that her father always believed that "you could accomplish anything you wanted if you really tried." His daughter proved him right.

With so many books to her credit, it's clear Naylor devotes a lot of time to her craft. "Even when I'm not writing, I'm thinking about what I'm working on or what I want to try next," Naylor says. But the author doesn't spend all her time writing. "I also take time to swim and hike and snorkel and eat Chinese food and chocolate and go to the theater and play the piano and visit schools and talk about my books," she says.

Naylor also enjoys a happy home life. She and Rex Naylor, a speech pathologist, have been married for more than forty years. The Naylors live in Bethesda, Maryland, and have two grown sons.

How *Shiloh* Came About

"You get a dog on your mind, it seems to fill up the whole space. Everything you do reminds you of that dog."

—Marty, Shiloh

What do you do if you find a stray dog that tears at your heart? If you're Phyllis Reynolds Naylor, you write about it.

Phyllis Reynolds Naylor met the dog that was to become Shiloh in much the same way that Marty does in Naylor's award-winning book.

"My husband and I were visiting friends in West Virginia," Naylor recalls, "and rose one morning for a long walk in the little community known as Shiloh." After passing the old gristmill, crossing the bridge, and walking just past the schoolhouse, they found a "hungry, trembling—and strangely silent—dog." The dog was too frightened to approach them until Naylor whistled. "When I whistled, it . . . came bounding over, leaping up to lick my cheek," Naylor says. "It followed us back to the house of our friends, and sat out all day in the rain, head on its paws, watching the door."

It was "the saddest dog I'd ever seen," Naylor says. And all that day she couldn't get the dog that was in the yard, in the rain, off her mind. She talked about it with her husband. She talked about it with their friends, Frank and Trudy Madden. They told her that the dog outside was just one of many that owners regularly abandoned in the West Virginia hills where they lived. Their words didn't make her feel any better.

Naylor left West Virginia that night with a heavy heart. "I agonized all the way back to Maryland that evening," she remembers. Her husband finally said to her, "Are you going to have a nervous breakdown or are you going to do something about it?" Naylor decided to do what she almost always did when faced with a difficult problem: write about it.

"I got hooked on that dog." Naylor remembers. "As Marty would say, [I was] whistling as though I meant something, then offering nothing. I felt I owed it more."

Naylor says she wrote the first draft of *Shiloh* at breakneck speed. "It was as though I was obsessed with getting to the end of the story and finding out just what happened between Marty and Judd Travers." The ending was difficult, though, because Naylor kept finding ways Judd might try to trick Marty. "I had to discover, like him, that nothing is as simple as you guess—not right or wrong, not Judd Travers, not even Marty himself or the dog," says Naylor. (The author eventually wrote two more Shiloh books, *Shiloh Season* and *Saving Shiloh*, in which she worked out some of her worries about Judd tricking Marty.)

The ending may not have been simple, but it was happy. Marty did get Shiloh. There was another happy ending, too. Just a few weeks after Naylor started writing *Shiloh,* she got a letter from her friends the Maddens. They had taken the abandoned dog into their home and named it Clover. Naylor remembered the kindness of her friends as well as the book's beginnings when she dedicated her book, "To Frank and Trudy Madden and a dog named Clover."

About *Shiloh*

◆ *You've said that you keep a notebook full of reference material for whatever book you're working on. Did you keep such a notebook for* Shiloh? *If so, what are some of the things it contained?*

No, not for *Shiloh*. Usually I think about a book months, even years, before I ever put a word down on paper. But it wasn't until I came across that sad, mistreated dog on a visit to West Virginia that the idea for a book took hold and wouldn't let go. I pushed all my other projects aside and started out cold, with not a note to my name. With the two sequels, however, my notebook included maps of the area, photos of Middle Island Creek, the old schoolhouse, and so on. I had to find out about West Virginia's hunting season, where the nearest jail was located, what the fine for hunting out of season would be, and all sorts of things that would help make the books authentic.

◆ *What prompted you to write sequels to* Shiloh?

First, I received interesting questions from readers. "How did Marty pay Doc Murphy for taking care of Shiloh after he was hurt?" And "Marty rescued one of Judd's dogs, but what happened to the rest?" However, what really made me want to write the sequels, after I had said there would never be a sequel to *Shiloh*, was that I received so many letters full of rage against Judd Travers. "Have Marty's father take a gun and shoot him through the eye," readers would write, ". . . through the brain, the heart, the ear. . . ." "Have Judd Travers go over the edge of a cliff and burn up," others wrote. I felt I could not leave readers with all that hate without giving them some understanding of how Judd got to be the way he was. And once we understand why people do what they do, it is easier to hope for redemption than to pray for revenge.

◆ *In your acceptance speech for the Newbery Medal [the medal awarded by the American Library Association for the most distinguished contribution to American literature for children], you said, "I had to discover, like [Marty], that nothing is as simple as you guess," which is what Marty says in the last paragraph of the book. Is this the main theme of the book?*

Yes, I think so. It is discovering that there is sometimes a very thin line between "right" and "wrong"—a vast gray area where rules and laws and moral concepts don't always tell you what you should do. There are times when you must simply think out a situation for yourself, and that's what Marty tries to do. One of the biggest rewards for me, in writing the Shiloh books, has been the number of librarians and teachers who tell me that these books provided some of the most stimulating conversations they have ever had in their classrooms. And the number of parents who had used the book as a read-aloud to their children, and had interesting family discussions as to what each member would do if confronted with Marty's dilemma.

◆ *What would you do if you were in Marty Preston's shoes and an abused dog ran away to you?*

That's exactly the question I asked myself when I found that dog, and the quest that prompted the book: What *would* I have done, especially if I were only eleven years old, in a small community where there was a strong tradition of individual rights, animal ownership, and minding your own business? And so I wrote the book to see how I would have handled it, were I in Marty's shoes.

About being a writer

◆ *You have said that on your deathbed you're sure you will gasp, "But I still have five more books to write!" Where do you get all of your ideas? How do you manage such a busy mind?*

It's hard, and almost makes me crazy. There are currently eight three-ring notebooks beside my writing chair, each with a title on masking tape stuck to the spine, waiting its turn. The notebooks were my husband's idea. I was going nuts trying to keep all this stuff in my head, afraid something would slip out and float away. Now, when I get another thought about a book-to-be, I simply open the notebook, jot it down, and can go back to the book I'm currently writing. I don't know where the ideas come from. They just do.

The more you write, the more possibilities you see for stories in things that happen to you, that people tell you, that you read about in the paper, or just imagine. In one way, all of these ideas are a blessing. I never have to go searching for something to write about. In another way, they're a curse, because the book you are *not* writing at the moment always seems better than the one that you are writing, and there's always that temptation to push one aside and start another.

◆ *How did it feel to win the Newbery Medal?*

What I remember most vividly was holding my stomach and bending over. Shock. I didn't even know it was being considered. In the middle of eating my shredded wheat, I was going over my writing tasks for the day, never dreaming that I would soon be on my way to New York for the *Today* show the following morning. It was certainly one of the most memorable times of my life, next to marrying my husband and giving birth to our sons. I wish that every author could experience the joy and wonder of the Newbery.

◆ *When do you write? Will you describe a typical day for us?*

I'm not happy unless I can spend a part of every day writing. It's sort of like steam building up inside my head, and writing helps release that. A usual day for me begins about 5:30 A.M., when I drive to an aquatics center near our house and do water-jogging for an hour. Or, if it's summer, I swim in our pool. After that, there's breakfast, a glance at the headlines, and then I begin, usually in my comfortable writing chair in the living room or a rocking chair on the screened porch. I often get in four to six hours, but the rest of the day is devoted to the business of writing—reading over contracts, answering questionnaires like this one, answering mail, looking over photo shoots for another dust jacket. I may take a walk at the end of the day or another swim, get dinner, write a little more if the writing is going well, watch *ER* or *West Wing* on TV, or go out to dinner and the theater with my husband.

◆ *How important is reading to your writing?*

It's not only interesting but professionally necessary to see how other writers deal with themes, or what voice works for a given novel. I have a much better ear than an eye, however. Perhaps because our parents read aloud to us until we were well into our teens, my ear seems able to pick up much more than my eye. I'm a very slow reader. And so I spend a considerable amount of money renting Books on Tape. The moment I get in my car, I "turn on" a novel. This is why it's easy for me to get up at 5:30 each morning. I can't wait to get in the car and "see what happens next."

◆ *What is your favorite thing about being a writer? What is your least favorite?*

The absolutely most favorite thing is the moment a character comes alive for me on paper, or where a place I am writing about suddenly seems real. There are no bands playing, no audience

15

applauding. It's a very solitary moment, but something akin to giving birth. "I've got it!" I say to myself, and from then on, the writing's a joy.

The least favorite is galley proofs. I'm actually not a very precise person. I would make a terrible accountant or rocket scientist or brain surgeon. And to have to go over every single word, every single punctuation mark . . . It's murder.

◆ *What do you find easiest when writing? What do you find hardest?*

Dialogue is the most fun for me, the easiest, and probably the most successful. Description is the hardest. I have to force myself to stop and describe something. I'm always afraid it's going to slow down the action, yet I love to read description in books by other authors. This probably has something to do with my ear being stronger than my eye.

◆ *What advice do you have for children who would like to be writers?*

When I speak in schools, I often give a writing workshop over a brown bag lunch to a dozen or so would-be writers. The question I am most often asked is, "I love to write, but I have a hard time thinking of something to write about. How do I get an idea?" And my answer is to think about the time in their lives when they were most sad, embarrassed, scared, or angry. Write down just a sentence or two about each of those episodes. Then, choose one, and turn it over to their imaginations. Give it wings. Make the beginning different. Change the ending. Have it happen to someone else. That way they are starting with something real that affected them deeply, and turning it into fiction.

General

◆ *If you weren't a writer, what might you be?*

It would have to be something I could hold in my hands. I like to make things, to have a finished product when I'm through. Perhaps I would be a baker and make bread. Or a weaver or a potter. I studied with the intent of becoming a psychologist and working with young children. And sometimes I wish I could have done that, too. But I think I made the right choice. Truly, I can't think of anything I would enjoy as much.

◆ *What's one thing, besides writing, that you're really good at? What's one thing that you're really bad at?*

I'm a good baker. I'm known for my poppyseed bread and Christmas cookies. At the opposite end of the scale, I'm also known for being the sloppiest bookkeeper. I have caused more messes in our checkbook than I would like to admit. But time will always be more important to me than money, and I can use every spare minute that I get.

These questions will help you think about the important parts of each chapter.

Chapter 1

- How do you know that Marty likes animals?
- Why isn't Marty's family allowed to have pets?
- What does it mean when Marty gives the dog a name?

Chapter 2

- How does Marty's dad react when Marty tells him Shiloh has ticks?
- If you were Marty, do you think you would be able to mind your own business regarding Judd and Shiloh?
- How would you feel about having to leave a dog with Judd Travers?

Chapter 3

- What does it say about Judd Travers's character that he doesn't name his dogs?
- Do you think Marty should have told Judd Travers that the dog's name was Shiloh? Why or why not?

Chapter 4

- Do you think Marty was right to take Shiloh and hide him? What would you have done?

- Marty does not bring Shiloh back to Judd as he said he would. Is it ever right to break a promise?
- After Shiloh returns, Marty sleeps through the night for the first time in a while. Why?

Chapter 5

- Do you think Marty is right to sneak food from his house for Shiloh?
- Judd Travers says, "He wasn't such a good hunting dog, I would have shot him by now." What do you think this comment will do to Marty's determination to keep Shiloh? What would you do?

Chapter 6

- Do you think it's okay to lie to some people but not to others? Is it okay for Marty to lie to Judd? Is it okay for him to lie to his family?
- What does Judd Travers tell Marty in this chapter that helps explain the man's character?
- Do you think Judd Travers is suspicious of Marty? Do you think you would be?

Chapter 7

- Why doesn't Marty tell David about Shiloh?
- After asking for more cookies for the walk home to give to Shiloh, Marty says to himself, "Seems I'm at the point where I'll do most anything for Shiloh . . . and right and wrong's all mixed up in my head." Do you think there are any easy answers for Marty? For anyone?

Chapter 8

- Marty thinks, "Having Shiloh a secret is like a bomb waiting to go off." Do you think all secrets are like that?
- What do you think is going to happen after Marty's mother finds Marty and Shiloh on the hill?

Chapter 9

- Do you think Marty's mother should tell his father about Shiloh?
- Why does Marty feel both relieved and scared that his mom found out about Shiloh?
- How do you think Marty feels about Shiloh getting hurt when he was supposed to be taking care of him?
- What do you think Marty's dad is going to do with the injured dog?

Chapter 10

- Why does Marty's dad make Marty tell Doc Murphy what happened?
- Why does Marty's dad think that Marty must be keeping other things from him?
- How do you know what's right and wrong? Do you agree with Marty's dad that you have to go by the law?

Chapter 11

- What are some of the bad things that resulted from Marty keeping Shiloh?
- How does Marty feel after he tells David all about Shiloh and what happened to him? Does having a friend to talk with usually make things easier?

Chapter 12

- Why did Marty's dad make him tell Judd Travers what happened when Judd came and found Shiloh in their house?
- Do you think there's any chance now that Judd will let Marty have the dog? Do you think there's any chance Marty will give him up? Can you imagine any solution to this problem?

Chapter 13

- Do you think Marty is wise to go alone to Judd Travers's place early in the morning? Do you think Judd would harm Marty?
- How might seeing Judd Travers shoot the young doe help Marty keep Shiloh?

Chapter 14

- Do you think it's right for Marty to blackmail Judd Travers in order to keep Shiloh?
- How is Marty putting other deer in danger by letting Judd get away with killing this doe?
- Marty says that this is and isn't the finest day in his life. Why?
- Do you think Marty's troubles with Judd are over?

Chapter 15

- Do you think Marty should have told his mother and father exactly what happened with Judd? What would you have told your parents if you were in Marty's position?
- Why does Marty feel sorry for Judd? Do you?
- Marty says, "Nothing is as simple as you guess." Do you agree? What happens between Marty and Shiloh to support this statement?

*"I'd got to the place I'd do most
anything to save Shiloh."*

—Marty, *Shiloh*

*S*hiloh is the story of a boy who falls in love with an abused dog and wants more than anything to make that dog safe, to make him his own.

Eleven-year-old Marty Preston is out walking near his home in the hills of West Virginia when he comes across a young beagle "not making any kind of noise, just slinking along with his head down, watching me, tail between his legs like he's hardly got the right to breathe." When Marty whistles and the beagle comes running to him, he and the dog become fast friends.

The dog follows him home, and Marty knows this means trouble. "We were never allowed to have pets. If you can't afford to feed 'em and take 'em to the vet when they're sick, you've no right taking 'em in, Ma says." Marty tells the dog to go home. But the dog won't leave. He lies down under a nearby sycamore tree. Later, when Marty sneaks to the window to see if the dog is still there, the beagle sees him and his tail starts to thump.

Marty is disappointed but not surprised when his father tells him that the dog is probably Judd Travers's new hunting dog and that they have to take him home. During the short ride over to Judd's, Marty wishes this dog belonged to anybody but Judd Travers. He doesn't like the man, and his dislike grows as they approach Judd's trailer and the dog starts trembling in Marty's lap.

"How do you go about reporting someone who don't take care of his dog right?" Marty asks. His dad tells him that many animals are mistreated. "But this one come to me to help him!" Marty says. His father reminds him that people in the hills mind their own business. "If it's Travers's dog, it's no mind of ours *how* he treats it."

When Judd welcomes his dog home with a kick, Marty jumps out of the Jeep. "Please don't kick him like that. Some dogs just like to run." Judd lets him know what he'll do if the dog does run again. "I'll whup the daylights out of him. Guarantee you that."

Marty can't speak all the way home. That night he decides he is going to buy the dog from Judd Travers. He doesn't know where he'll get the money, he doesn't know if Judd will sell, he doesn't know what his parents will say or how he'll get the money to feed a dog, but buying him is the only way he can figure to get the dog away from Judd.

Then Shiloh runs away from Judd again, this time straight to Marty's house, and Marty hides the dog in a pen he builds on a hill behind his house.

At first, Marty finds it easy to keep Shiloh a secret. But it involves more and more lies. And the lying only begins with Judd, who comes looking for the dog one night and leaves without him. Marty lies to his parents, his siblings, and his best friend. He can't seem to help himself. "A lie don't seem a lie anymore when it's meant to save a dog," he thinks, "and right and wrong's all mixed up in my head."

Then one night Marty's mother follows him up the hill after dinner and finds him lying in the pen with Shiloh.

"I wish you'd told me," his mother says. Marty says she'd make him give the dog back, and she reminds him that the dog isn't his. Marty's mother wants to tell his father about the dog, but agrees to wait a day if Marty promises not to run away.

That night Marty hears Shiloh up on the hill. It's clear that he's being hurt. Marty runs up the hill with his father behind him. His father shines a flashlight on the pen. A big, mean German shepherd with blood on his mouth is hunched over Shiloh. The big dog jumps over the fence and runs away. Shiloh, unmoving, is covered with blood.

Marty's dad carries Shiloh to his Jeep. Marty gets in beside him, and they drive to Doc Murphy's. The doctor examines Shiloh while Marty explains who the dog is and what happened. Doc Murphy cleans the wounds, stitches Shiloh, and gives him antibiotics. "The next twenty-four hours, we'll know if this dog's going to live," he says.

Marty asks his father if he can still keep Shiloh. His father says no, that they can only keep him until he is well. "Then we're taking him back to Judd."

Doc Murphy brings Shiloh back the next day. Marty and his family bring the dog into the house and make him a bed in a cardboard box. Marty is very happy to have Shiloh there, in the house. Then Judd knocks on their door one night during dinner. "Ray Preston, somebody told me you got my dog."

Marty's dad makes Marty tell how Shiloh came to be there and how he got hurt. Judd is angry. Marty's dad says what Marty did was wrong, and he'll pay the doctor's bill and make sure the dog is well before returning him. Then Marty's mother asks if they can buy the dog. "That dog's not for sale," Judd says. "I want him back by Sunday."

But Marty isn't willing to let Shiloh go. He decides that the only thing he can do is go and talk to Judd and tell him he won't give Shiloh back. He goes to tell him early Sunday morning. The boy is on his way to Judd's when he sees a young doe shot and killed. Who is shooting deer out of season? Marty wonders. Then he sees Judd Travers stepping out of the woods.

Marty tells Judd he saw what happened, and that there is a two-hundred-dollar fine for killing a doe. Marty says he'll tell the warden unless Judd lets him keep Shiloh. Judd only agrees to the deal if Marty will work twenty hours at his place to pay for the dog as well. Marty quickly consents to this plan.

When he gets back to his house, Marty tells his mom and dad that Shiloh is going to be his. He tells them how he's going to work twenty hours to pay Judd for Shiloh. Marty doesn't tell them about the deer.

Marty goes to Judd's two hours a day for the next two weeks. Judd is cruel and makes Marty work in the hot sun, seldom offering him anything to drink. Marty doesn't care, though. His mind is focused on one thing: owning Shiloh.

By Thursday of the last week, it is clear Marty has won Shiloh with his hard work and determination. When it's time to leave that last day, Judd gives Marty an old dog collar. "You got yourself a dog," Judd says.

That night Marty lies on the grass with Shiloh on top of him. He looks up at the sky and thinks "how nothing is as simple as you guess—not right or wrong, not Judd Travers, not even me or this dog I got here. But the good part is I saved Shiloh and opened my eyes some. Now that ain't bad for eleven."

Thinking about the plot
• Why did Marty want Shiloh so badly? Why couldn't he have him?
• How did Marty try to keep Shiloh?
• How did Marty finally get Shiloh?

"You live in hill country, it takes a while for the sun to rise. Got to scale the mountains first."

—Marty, *Shiloh*

Shiloh takes place in Friendly, West Virginia, some time during the mid- to late-twentieth century. The setting is rural—it takes place in the countryside—and poor.

The author establishes the rural setting in a number of ways. She describes where the Prestons live, where Marty finds Shiloh, and where Marty and Shiloh play. She tells about Marty's father's job. She talks about the characters' activities and pastimes. And she has them speak in a rural West Virginia dialect (see page 29).

Marty and his family live up in the hills above Friendly, West Virginia. Friendly is near Sistersville, which is halfway between Wheeling and Parkersburg. The Prestons live in a four-room house that is surrounded on three sides by hills. Marty loves the hills, and the animals he can see there.

Much of the story takes place in these hills. There are woods, a creek, and a meadow. It is on one of the hills that Marty builds a pen and hides Shiloh. The boy and dog run and play on this hill. And it is there that Shiloh is attacked and nearly killed by Baker's German shepherd.

Marty finds Shiloh down by the old Shiloh schoolhouse, by the road that follows the slow-moving river. There are some houses along this road, but not many.

Marty's father is a rural mail carrier. Mr. Preston uses his Jeep to deliver mail to two hundred families in Sistersville and two hundred families in Friendly. By Marty's estimate, his dad travels eighty-five miles a day to make these deliveries. Many miles of these country roads are impassable in winter.

Rural activities and pastimes play an important part in this book. Hunting, which can only take place in the country, is an important part of the story: Judd Travers bought Shiloh because he was a good hunting dog; Marty catches Judd Travers hunting out of season, thereby paving the way for him to blackmail Judd to sell him Shiloh; even Marty, though he doesn't hunt, owns a gun and uses it for target practice.

The countryside is also a great place to play: Marty and his best friend, David, like to run on the hills behind Marty's house; Marty's sisters like to catch fireflies outside the house. Finally, it is a place with enough land for gardens and animals: Marty's mother and Judd Travers both have vegetable gardens and Marty's family even keeps hens.

The author further establishes *Shiloh*'s setting by having her characters speak in a West Virginia regional dialect. This means that the characters' vocabulary, grammar, and pronunciation are unique to the area in which they live. We hear this dialect from the beginning, in the first sentence of the book when Marty says, "The day Shiloh come, we're having us a big Sunday dinner." The use of dialect helps us *hear* where the story is taking place.

The setting of *Shiloh* is poor as well as rural. The author both shows us and tells us of the poverty of the area. When Marty is looking for a job, his father tells him that he doesn't know many folks with money to spare. And when Marty applies to be a newspaper carrier, there are already six other names on the list—and one is a grown man with a car.

Marty's family is also poor. Though Marty's father has a job as a mail carrier—one of the better paying jobs in rural areas—the family struggles financially. They live in a small, four-room house, and Marty's bed is on the couch in the living room. Marty's mother does laundry using an old washing machine with a wringer that only works if you turn it by hand. The Prestons don't even have a telephone; if they want to make a call, they have to go to Doc Murphy's house. And when Dara Lynn outgrows her sneakers, Mrs. Preston cuts the tops off to make room for her toes until they can afford a new pair.

The story of the love between a boy and a dog is timeless, and the author doesn't give the reader many hints as to the exact time that this story takes place. The book was published in 1991, and it is not at all futuristic, so it's safe to guess that it takes place before 1991. The existence of Jeeps, televisions, and telephones could place it as early as the mid-twentieth century.

Thinking about the setting
• Where does *Shiloh* take place?
• When does *Shiloh* take place?
• What is dialect? How does the author's use of dialect help establish the story's setting?

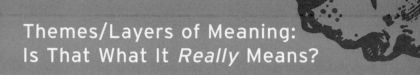

"Nothing is as simple as you guess—not right or wrong, not Judd Travers, not even me or this dog I got here."

—Marty, *Shiloh*

These words—among the last in *Shiloh*—express the overriding theme of the book: that right and wrong are not always clear-cut, not always black and white; instead, right and wrong are often different shades of gray.

According to the author, *Shiloh* deals with the difficulty of making ethical decisions in complex situations. "Much of life is, of necessity, compromise," Naylor has said. "When should he [Marty] give in, and for what principles should he hold out? Where is the dividing line between lawful duty and being true to one's conscience? Between loyalty to one's family and the love of a dog?"

Marty struggles with these questions throughout the book. In the beginning, when Shiloh follows Marty home, the boy wants to feed him. But Marty's mother has often said that they can't have a pet because they can't afford to feed it. Marty thinks about trying to sneak Shiloh some of his dinner anyway, but his mother is watching him too closely. She tells him that he'd better not feed his dinner to the dog; if Marty doesn't want his dinner, his father can take it to work the next day for lunch. So Marty excuses himself, goes out, takes an egg from one of the hen's nests, and feeds it to Shiloh. Already he is doing something he knows he shouldn't be doing—taking away from his family to feed the dog.

Even when he's just thinking about trying to buy Shiloh from Judd, Marty knows that feeding him will be a problem. "There aren't many leftover scraps of anything in our house. Every extra bite of pork chop or boiled potato or spoonful of peas gets made into soup," he says. He wants Shiloh so badly, he refuses to think about how he might feed him once he gets him. "I figure to get to that problem later on," he says.

But Marty has to face that problem—and a host of others—sooner than he realizes, because Shiloh shows up outside his house the next day. Marty's first decision puts him in that gray area between right and wrong: He decides not to bring Shiloh back to Judd Travers.

"I don't have time to think how I had promised Judd if I ever saw Shiloh loose again, I'd bring him back," Marty thinks. "Don't even think what I'm going to tell Dad. All I know right then is that I have to get Shiloh away from the house, where none of the family will see him."

Why does Marty break his promise to Judd Travers and begin deceiving his family? In his eyes, it's the only way he can protect Shiloh. "I'm not never going to let anybody hurt him again ever," he says to himself. Marty has to do what he knows is wrong in order to do what he believes is right.

The next day is filled with lies—both to Judd Travers and to his family. Marty doesn't have too much trouble lying to Judd. He makes up a prayer to justify not being honest with the man about Shiloh. "Jesus," he says, "which you want me to do? Be one hundred percent honest and carry that dog back to Judd so that one of your creatures can be kicked and starved all over again, or keep him here and fatten him up to glorify your creation?"

"The problem's more mixed up than that, though," Marty thinks. "I'm lying to my folks as well." Marty sees that life is full of trade-offs. "I'm *not* eating the leftover meat loaf I've put away. Every bit of food saved is money saved that could go to buy Dara Lynn a new pair of sneakers so Ma won't have to cut open the tops of her old ones to give her toes more room," he thinks. But he convinces himself that he's not taking anything away from the family, because he's giving Shiloh food from his own plate.

Marty is hungry all the time because he's giving Shiloh half his food. So when he goes to visit his friend David Howard, he eats his fill at lunch and then asks Mrs. Howard for food for the walk home. The food is really for Shiloh. Marty thinks, "Ma would have blushed with shame if she heard me ask this, but seems I'm at the point where I'll do most anything for Shiloh. A lie don't seem a lie anymore when it's meant to save a dog, and right and wrong's all mixed up in my head."

Marty also learns that the simple things he does for Shiloh—
telling David his mother has headaches so he shouldn't come
over, going to the corner grocer and asking Mr. Wallace if he has
any old food he can buy, cheap—have repercussions for the whole
family. The townspeople ask Marty's mother how she's feeling
and offer her headache remedies. When she shops, she finds
everything she wants is on sale. And people start leaving food for
Marty's dad in their mailboxes. In his attempts to protect and care
for Shiloh, Marty entangles his family in a web of deceit.

When his mother discovers Marty and Shiloh on the hill, Marty begs
her not to tell his dad about it until the next day. She reluctantly
agrees. When he finds out, it causes trouble between them.

And then Marty has to face the worst result of his hiding Shiloh:
The beagle is attacked in his pen by a big German shepherd.
"Worst of all," Marty thinks, "I'd brought Shiloh here to keep him
from being hurt, and what that German shepherd done to him
was probably worse than anything Judd Travers would have
brought himself to do, short of shootin' him anyways."

Marty's dad is angry about Marty secretly keeping Shiloh. And,
though Marty understands his dad's anger, he's angry, too. He
wants his dad to understand that "it's not all so black and white"
as he makes it out to be.

"You would have thought more of me if I'd let that dog wander
around till Judd found it again, kick the daylights out of 'im?"
Marty asks his dad.

"I want you to do what's right," his dad tells him.

"What's right?" Marty asks.

His father knows that there are no clear answers to this, but finally says, "You've got to go by the law. The law says a man that pays money for a dog owns that dog. You don't agree with the law, then you work to change it."

But Marty refuses to give up. "What if there isn't time, Dad? Shiloh could be dead by the time somebody looked into the way Judd treats his dogs."

Right and wrong aren't black and white, they're shades of gray.

Marty is caught in these gray areas again when he sees Judd shoot a deer out of season. "One way you look at it," Marty thinks, "it's my duty to report a killed doe. The way folks up here look at it, though, that's snitching. And if I *might* could tell, but bargain not to, it's something else again: It's blackmail." Marty knows that none of these choices is perfect. But he must choose and, in the end, he chooses blackmail. "Like I said," he thinks, "I'd got to the place I'd do most anything to save Shiloh."

Marty knows his choice is as much wrong as right. Marty knows "that by lettin' him get away with this, I'm putting other deer in danger." Marty reminds himself that he's doing this for Shiloh, and puts these thoughts out of his head.

But his conscience still troubles him. "I begin to see now that I'm no better than Judd Travers—willing to look the other way to get something I want," he says.

Marty and Judd make an agreement that Marty will work twenty hours to pay for Shiloh. Judd is mean to Marty, and at times it looks like Judd isn't going to stick to his end of the bargain. But, in the end, he does. And he gives Marty an old collar for Shiloh. This kindness, coming from Judd, surprises Marty, who summarizes the main theme of the book: "I'm thinking how nothing is as simple as you guess—not right or wrong, not Judd Travers, not even me or this dog I got here."

Honesty

Another important theme in the book is honesty. Marty gets himself and his family into trouble by being dishonest about Shiloh.

Marty knows that it's wrong to lie. He lied once about eating the ear of Dara Lynn's chocolate Easter rabbit, and felt awful about it. He knows he shouldn't be lying now, but can't think of any other way to save Shiloh.

Marty's dishonesty takes two forms. First, there are the "flat-out lies." Marty lies about what he's doing with the food he sets aside from dinner, saying he's saving it for when he's hungry later, when he's really saving it for Shiloh; he lies when he tells his parents that there's nothing for his friend David to do on the hill, when he knows there's lots for David to do; Marty lies when he tells Dara Lynn that he saw "the biggest, meanest snake" on the hill that morning, just to keep Dara Lynn from following him and finding Shiloh. These are examples of Marty's outright lies.

Then there is the dishonesty that Marty describes as lying "not only by what you say but what you don't say." This is called lying by omission, by not telling the whole truth. One of many instances in which Marty tells this type of lie is when Judd comes to the Prestons looking for his dog, and Marty says he hasn't seen him in their yard that day. "That was the honest-to-God truth," Marty thinks, "because Shiloh hadn't been anywhere near our yard." But Marty knows he has lied to Judd, because "what I'd kept inside myself made him think that I hadn't seen his dog at all," when, in fact, Marty had just come from playing with Shiloh on the hill behind the house.

Marty begins lying so much that it becomes "easy as falling off a log." When Marty's mother discovers his secret, he begs her not to tell his dad, at least not until the next day. But Marty's mother is reluctant to agree to this.

"I never kept a secret from your dad in the fourteen years we've been married," she says.

"You ain't going to tell him?" Marty says.

"Marty, I've got to," she says. "He ever finds out about this dog and knows I knew but didn't tell him, how could he trust me? I keep this one secret from him, he'll think maybe there are more."

And she's right. When Marty's dad finds out about Shiloh, he's angry at Marty and at his wife for keeping the dog a secret.

"Marty," his dad says to him, "what else don't I know?... You keeping Judd's dog up there on our hill.... What else you keeping from me?"

"*Nothing*, Dad!" Marty says.

"How do I know that's not another lie?"

"'Cause it's not."

"You saying so don't make it true."

Marty later hears his mother and father talking late into the night. He hears his father questioning his mother, upset that she kept this secret from him.

Even when Marty makes a deal with Judd to work to buy Shiloh, he realizes how much damage dishonesty can do. "You've got my word," Marty says to Judd. Then he adds, to himself, "which, considering all the lying I'd been doing lately, didn't seem like it amounted to much."

Responsibility

Responsibility is another important theme in the book. Marty has a responsibility to his family, to Shiloh, to society, and to his conscience. He also must take responsibility for his actions.

Marty's responsibility to his family is to do what he can to help the family and to obey his parents' rules. He does this without much difficulty until Shiloh appears. Then he begins giving food to Shiloh that he should be eating. But he knows that if he takes extra, "then it means Shiloh's costing us money we can't afford." Marty knows that he is potentially causing his family a lot of trouble by hiding Shiloh. But the responsibility he feels for the dog is greater than what he feels for his family.

Marty feels obligated to help Shiloh. He feels bad after he takes him back to Judd the first time, feels that he let the dog down. "I'd disappointed him," he says, "whistling like I meant something that first time, gettin' him to come to me, then taking him on back to Judd Travers to be kicked all over again." Marty believes Shiloh needs him, "needs me bad." So when Shiloh comes back to him, Marty says, "He's my dog now, and I'm not never going to let anybody hurt him again ever."

In order to fulfill the responsibility he feels for Shiloh, Marty must also ignore his responsibility to society. He ignores the rules of behavior in Tyler County, that "around here folks keep to their own business." He ignores the law by taking another man's dog.

Finally, Marty must take responsibility for his own actions. When Shiloh is attacked by the German shepherd and Marty and his dad bring the dog to Doc Murphy's, it's Marty, not his dad, who has to tell the doctor that this is Judd Travers's dog. It is also Marty who is going to have to figure out a way to pay Doc Murphy for fixing up Shiloh. And when Judd Travers finds his dog at the Prestons', it's Marty who has to explain to him how he got there. And, in the end, it's Marty who works for Judd to pay for the dog.

Dogs

Another theme running through the book is that there's nothing like the love of a dog. Marty thinks, "Nobody loves you as much as a dog. Except your ma, maybe." And his parents, though they know that having a dog is an expense they really can't afford, are nearly as delighted as Marty that Shiloh is theirs. As Marty's dad says, "There's food for the body and food for the spirit. And Shiloh sure enough feeds our spirit."

Thinking about the themes

- What is the main theme of Shiloh? What are some other themes in the book?
- Do you agree with Marty that "nothing is as simple as you guess"? What experiences have you had in which right and wrong were not black and white, but shades of gray?
- How important is honesty? Do you think Marty was wrong to lie? Is it ever right to lie?
- What do you think Marty's primary responsibilities are? What are yours?
- Do you agree that there is nothing like the love of a dog?

There are about a dozen characters in this book. The main characters are Marty Preston, Shiloh, and Judd Travers.

Here is a list of characters, followed by a brief description of each of the most significant ones.

Marty Preston	an eleven-year-old boy
Shiloh	the beagle Marty rescues
Judd Travers	Shiloh's owner
Lou Preston/Ma	Marty's mother
Ray Preston/Dad	Marty's father
Dara Lynn	Marty's seven-year-old sister
Becky	Marty's three-year-old sister
David Howard	Marty's friend
Mrs. Howard	David's mother
Doc Murphy	the neighborhood doctor
Mr. Wallace	the corner storekeeper
Baker's German shepherd	a dog that attacks Shiloh

Marty Preston: Marty, the main character in the book, is an eleven-year-old boy who respects his parents, understands his responsibility to his family, loves animals, and thinks he lives in the best place in the world. Marty also has a keen sense of justice and is willing to take risks for what he wants, and for what he believes is right.

That Marty respects his parents is clear from the beginning of the book. When Marty remembers his mother's words—that if you can't afford to feed an animal and take it to a vet when it's sick, you have no right taking it in—he tells Shiloh to go home, even though he's already fond of the dog and would love a pet. And he gets in the Jeep to return Shiloh to Judd when his father tells him to, even though he doesn't want to go.

Marty also knows his responsibility to his family. When he is trying to think of ways to make money, he remembers reading about kids earning money baby-sitting. Even though he baby-sits his younger sisters a lot, he says it would never occur to him to ask for pay. He knows if he asked, his dad would say, "You live in this house, boy? Then you do your share like the rest of us."

We learn of Marty's love for animals on page one, when he can't eat his fried rabbit after learning that the animal didn't die right away when his father shot it. Then Marty goes out with his .22 rifle and says that he will shoot at an apple or a row of cans. "Never shoot at anything moving, though," he thinks. "Never had the slightest wish." Marty's love of animals is also expressed in his desire to be a vet one day. Finally, Marty shows his love of animals in the way he takes care of Shiloh—risking trouble for himself and his family, and going without half his food, to save the dog from abuse.

Marty also loves where he lives. He expresses this love after he reveals that his father told him that Sistersville was one of the best places to live in the whole state. "You ask *me* the best place to live, I'd say right where we are, a little four-room house with hills on three sides."

Marty's keen sense of justice is evident throughout the book. It's evident when his father makes him take Shiloh back after he first finds him, and Marty wants to report Judd for not taking care of his dog. It's evident when his mother finds him with Shiloh up on the hill and tells him that, in the eyes of the law, the dog belongs to Judd. "What kind of a law is it, Ma, that lets a man mistreat his dog?" he asks. Marty also shows his strong sense of justice after he sees Judd shoot the doe. He thinks about how people are supposed to mind their own business, and wonders if that is always right. Marty thinks, "Wonder if Dad wouldn't never tell on Judd no matter what he done. Bet he would. There's got to be times that what one person does is everybody's business."

Shiloh: The beagle that Marty first sees down by the old Shiloh schoolhouse is also one of the main characters in the book. The young dog—Marty guesses he's a year or two old—is scared, but when he learns to trust, he is very loving and friendly. Shiloh is smart. He also likes to run "all over creation," as Judd tells Marty when the boy returns the dog to his owner.

When Marty first sees Shiloh, he describes him as "just slinking along with his head down, watching me, tail between his legs like he's hardly got the right to breathe." When Marty walks toward him, the dog backs off. Marty says that when you see a dog cringe like that, "you know somebody's been kicking at him. Beating on him maybe." This mistreatment is confirmed when Marty and his dad return Shiloh and, as soon as Shiloh leaps onto the ground, he "connects with Judd's right foot."

The dog remembers Marty's kindness, and runs away to Marty's house the next time Judd takes him out hunting. When Marty tells Shiloh to be quiet, that he can't let his family hear him, the dog seems to understand. He lets Marty carry him up the hill and doesn't make a sound. And he doesn't make a sound when he's left alone in his pen, either. The only time he makes any noise that would give him away is when he's attacked by Baker's German shepherd.

Shiloh shows how loving and friendly he is from the beginning. When Marty first whistles for him, "It's like pressing a magic button," Marty thinks. "The beagle comes barreling toward me, legs going lickety-split, long ears flopping, tail sticking up like a flagpole. . . ." And his tail, when it's not tucked between his legs in fear of Judd Travers, is always wagging, like a propeller or a windshield wiper.

Judd Travers: Judd Travers, Marty's neighbor and Shiloh's owner, is another main character in the book. First we hear from Marty why Judd is not a likable character. Then, after we meet Judd, we learn to dislike him on our own.

Marty states his reasons for disliking Judd in the beginning of the book. The first of these is that Judd mistreats his dogs. In addition, Marty has seen the man cheat Mr. Wallace at the cash register. He has also caught Judd killing deer out of season.

We first meet Judd when Marty and his dad return Shiloh. We hear Judd curse, yell at the dog, kick him, and promise to whip him if he runs off again. Marty's description seems just right.

We also get a glimpse of Judd's interests by reading what magazines he gets. The day that Marty and his dad deliver the Sears fall catalog, Judd doesn't get a copy, but he does get two magazines—*Guns and Ammo* and *Shooting Times.*

Even though Judd is an unlikable character, the author keeps us from truly hating him by giving us information that helps explain why Judd is the way he is. Judd tells Marty at one point, "Far back as I can remember, Pa took the belt to me—big old welts on my back so raw I could hardly pull my shirt back on." Later, when Marty asks Judd if his father took him out hunting when he was little, Judd answers, "Once or twice. Only nice thing about my dad I remember." And Marty feels sorry for Judd Travers. Readers do, too.

By the end, we see that Judd can be nice. He's mostly mean to Marty while he's working to pay for Shiloh. Sometimes, though, Judd gives Marty water. And, after Shiloh is paid for, Judd gives Marty a collar for the dog.

Lou Preston/Ma: Marty's mother is also an important character in the book. She is a very practical person; with money tight, she has to be. When Marty first finds Shiloh and the dog follows him home, Marty hears his mother's practical voice in his head saying that if you can't afford to care for an animal, you have no right taking it in.

Marty's mother is also very perceptive and observant. She can tell just by looking at Marty that he is still thinking about Shiloh. And she is the only one to suspect that Marty is saving food from dinner for someone other than himself.

When Marty's mother finds Shiloh and Marty together, she tells him, "I never kept a secret from your dad in the fourteen years we've been married." But she is willing to keep Shiloh a secret for one day as long as Marty promises not to run away. Her son's safety is more important than anything else.

In the end, Marty's mother is as softhearted as she is practical. She can't bear to see Judd take Shiloh back and, even though there's little money to spare, she asks Judd if they can buy the dog. When Marty finally earns the dog, Ma bakes a chocolate layer cake to celebrate. "A real cake, too, not no Betty Crocker," Marty thinks, showing just how special his mom and everyone else think Shiloh is.

Ray Preston/Dad: Marty's father, another important character in the book, repeatedly tells Marty to "keep to your own business." When Marty worries that Shiloh has been mistreated, his dad tells him, "If it's Travers's dog, it's no mind of ours how he treats it." Having said that, Ray Preston later asks Judd how the dogs are, and reminds him that he's got to keep them healthy if he wants to have them around for a while. He does this for Marty's sake, because he knows how his son cares for Shiloh.

Ray Preston is a firm believer in personal responsibility. When he and Marty take Shiloh to Doc Murphy's, the father makes his son tell the doctor what happened. And when Judd comes storming to their house because he's heard Shiloh is there, Ray makes Marty explain how Shiloh came to be there, and how he was hurt.

Like many people, Marty's dad tends to see things in black and white; something's right or wrong, there's no middle ground. After leaving Shiloh with Doc Murphy, Ray Preston tells Marty that he wants him to do what's right. When Marty asks him what's right, his dad is momentarily stumped. Marty, who sees the gray areas between black and white, wants his dad to see them, too.

Every night after dinner, Ray Preston goes out to look at the sky; he knows there's more to life than hard work. So it's not such a surprise at the end of the book when he says, after worrying about how they can afford to feed Shiloh, "But there's food for the body and food for the spirit. And Shiloh sure enough feeds our spirit."

Thinking about the characters

- In your own words, how would you describe Marty Preston? Do you think you would like to be friends with a boy like Marty? Why or why not?
- How does the author show us that Shiloh has been abused?
- How does the author keep Marty's character from being all good, and Judd's from being all bad?

It's a winner!

Shiloh is a winner—a Newbery Award winner, that is. Phyllis
Reynolds Naylor won the 1992 Newbery Medal for *Shiloh*. The
Newbery is a very prestigious honor: It is given annually by the
children's librarians of the American Library Association to the
author of "the most distinguished contribution to American literature
for children" published the preceding year. Look at your copy of
Shiloh and you might see the award, printed in gold on the cover.

In addition to being a big hit with the fifteen librarians on the
Newbery Committee, *Shiloh* was and is a big hit with kids. The
book continues to be popular more than ten years after it was
first published. *Shiloh* is so popular, in fact, that Phyllis Reynolds
Naylor wrote two sequels, and the original and the first sequel
have been made into movies.

Does the dialect add to or take away from your understanding?

Despite *Shiloh*'s popularity, there have been a few criticisms of
the book. Most reviewers liked the use of dialect. One reviewer
wrote, "The book is filled with West Virginia dialect, furthering
the strong and well-defined sense of place." But another wrote,

"Readers may have difficulty understanding some of the first-person narration as it is written in rural West Virginian dialect."

Is this boy for real?

Another criticism of the book is that the character of Marty Preston seems too good to be true. These critics argue that Marty's decision to follow his conscience, to tell Judd he's not giving Shiloh back, even though this decision might involve personal risk, is not normal behavior for an eleven-year-old boy. "Most adults, let alone children, do not operate at this high level" of moral behavior, the critics argue. They do not say that this takes away from the value of the book, however. "We believe that what Marty does for readers, particularly children, is provide them with an example of what they can aspire to become," one critic writes.

Thinking about what others think about *Shiloh*

- Do you think that *Shiloh* seems like an award-winning book? What other Newbery Award–winning books have you read? How does *Shiloh* compare?

- What do you think of the author's use of West Virginia dialect in *Shiloh*? Do you think it adds to or detracts from the book? Did you find it difficult to read?

- Do you think Marty Preston's moral behavior is too mature for an eleven-year-old boy? Why or why not? Do you think it harms the book in any way if it is? Do you think it's good to read about characters who provide you with an example of what you can try to become?

abandon to leave forever

antibiotic a drug, such as penicillin, that kills bacteria and is used to cure infections and disease

blackmail to threaten to reveal a secret about someone unless the person pays a sum of money or grants a favor

commences begins

cringe to shrink in fear

decency respectable and proper behavior

detour a longer alternative route usually taken when the direct route is closed for repairs

enthusiasm great excitement or interest

envy to wish that you could have something that another person has or do something that he or she has done

grovel to be unnaturally humble and polite to someone because you are afraid of the person or because you think he or she is very important

gunnysack a sack made of coarse heavy fabric

investigator someone who finds out as much as possible about something

jubilation great happiness and delight

lard a solid, white grease, made from the melted fat of pigs and hogs, that is used in cooking

mournful feeling, showing, or filled with grief

omission the act of leaving something out

parlor a formal living room

quavery shaky

remedy something that relieves pain, cures a disease, or corrects a disorder

slog to work hard and steadily

snarl to growl angrily

snitch to be a tattletale

stethoscope a medical instrument used by doctors and nurses to listen to the sounds from a patient's heart, lungs, and other areas

suspicious distrustful; thinking that something is wrong, with little or no proof to back up these feelings

sympathy the understanding and sharing of other people's troubles

turpentine a thin distilled oil used as a paint thinner, solvent, and liniment

warble to sing with trills, runs, or other melodic sounds

warden an official who is responsible for enforcing certain laws

whetstone a stone for sharpening tools

wince to flinch or shrink back because you are in pain, embarrassed, or disgusted

Phyllis Reynolds Naylor on Writing

Phyllis Reynolds Naylor's husband has said of his wife, "Writing is as necessary for her as eating or sleeping." Naylor agrees. "I'm not happy unless I spend some time every day writing."

Where does Naylor get her ideas? Early in her writing career, she used to go to a quiet place with a pad of paper and brainstorm things to write about. Now she struggles to keep all the ideas that pop into her head from overwhelming her. She deals with this by starting a notebook for each of her book ideas. "Every time I get an idea about one of these books, I jot it down in the notebook," she says. "There are pockets in each notebook which I fill with photographs, maps, pages from the telephone book, newspaper clippings—anything at all that will help me in the writing of the book."

These notebooks let Naylor concentrate on what she's working on without worrying about forgetting other good ideas she has. They also give her plenty to choose from when she is ready to begin writing a new book. Naylor says that at any given time she might have as many as ten of these notebooks on a shelf beside her writing chair.

Naylor's books are set in all sorts of places, from West Virginia to Maryland to England. The only criteria Naylor uses for choosing a setting is that she has to know it. As a result, many of her books are set in places where she has lived or visited often.

The themes for Naylor's books are usually serious. That's because, Naylor says, "these are the kinds of books I most like to write, serious themes with a lot of hope, humor, poignancy. Because, when you come right down to it, that's the way I see life." The author has also found that she likes to write about regular people. "I love to write about ordinary people in extraordinary situations," she says. Another favorite is poor people, because, she says, "I just feel that poor people are far more creative in some ways than people who have all the advantages."

Naylor doesn't base her characters on specific people, though her characters may possess traits of people she knows, even family members. When Naylor "gives birth" to a character, as she describes it, she begins by writing a character sketch for that character. "I think about them a long time," she says. "I imagine them in various situations and how they would feel." Even with her character sketches, however, Naylor doesn't feel that she knows her characters until she starts writing about them. "You don't *really* know your character until you see him there on the pages," she says.

Naylor spends most of her waking moments writing or thinking about writing, and she wouldn't have it any other way. "There is no other job I would enjoy so much, for in my books I can be anyone I please—old or young, boy or girl. I can do wildly exciting things I would never dream of doing in real life, and can experience sorrows and terrors that I have always been curious about."

Naylor can't imagine not writing. "I will go on writing because an idea in the head is like a rock in the shoe; I just can't wait to get it out." And Naylor has lots of ideas. She is sure that her dying words will be, "But I still have five more books to write!"

For aspiring writers

Naylor stresses the value of perseverance for all writers. In the course of publishing more than one hundred books and two thousand stories and articles, Naylor has received more than ten thousand rejection letters. She received a lot of these rejections early on, before she started writing books. But she didn't let them stop her, they only spurred her to do better. "If I hadn't stuck with it," she says, "if I hadn't tried to make my next story better than the one before, I probably wouldn't ever have got up the courage to write books."

The author offers this final word of advice to aspiring writers: "Write the story only you can write—something you can really love or feel." That's what Naylor does, and it's clearly a winning formula.

You Be the Author!

- **Character sketch:** Naylor usually writes a character sketch for all her characters. A character sketch tells everything you might want to know about the character—even if you never use the information in a story. For instance, it might tell what a character looks like, when his birthday is, what his favorite color is, whether he keeps his room neat or messy, what he likes to do in his spare time, what kind of music he likes, who his friends— and his enemies—are. A character sketch also shows the character in different situations, exploring how he might act and feel, even if you don't use those situations in your story.

Think of a story you'd like to write. Who are the characters? Write a character sketch for each.

- **A different ending:** Naylor had a tough time finishing *Shiloh*. "At every turn, it seemed, in the final chapters and in subsequent drafts," she said, "I found still another way that Judd might try to trick Marty, another way that Marty could win and yet lose at the same time."

Can you imagine a different ending for *Shiloh*? There are lots of possibilities. Think of one, then write it.

• **Pay attention:** Naylor is able to tell stories that seem quite real because she pays attention to what's happening around her. "When I'm out in public," she says, "I really pay attention . . . I'm always listening."

You can become a better writer by learning to pay attention. Starting right now, make it a point to pay special attention to all you see and hear around you. At the end of each day, come home and write what you remember about your day. What did you see? What did you hear? Your ability to pay attention will improve with practice—as will your writing!

• **Keep a notebook:** While you don't need to keep a notebook for every story idea you have, as Naylor does, it is a good idea to keep a notebook in which you can jot down ideas for stories, characters, dialogue, and settings as they come to you. That way, when you're ready to write, you'll have a treasure trove of ideas from which to choose.

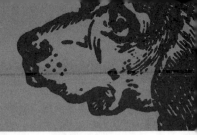

- **Book it:** As you read earlier, Phyllis Reynolds Naylor "published" her first books when she was in fourth grade. "I was the author, illustrator, printer, binder, and librarian, all in one," she said. You can do the same.

First, write a story. (For tips on writing a story, see page 54.) Then, decide how you want to divide your story into sections. You might do this by figuring how much writing you want on each page, or by deciding where you want to include illustrations—at the beginning, in the middle, on every page, wherever you want. Then, print or type the story. Draw your illustrations. Give the book a cover that will grab the reader's attention, and staple the whole thing together. You can use masking tape or a strip of colored paper to make a binding, as the young Naylor did. And, if you want to be librarian, too, glue half of an old envelope into the back of your book so you can put cards in it to let you know where the book is, and let the borrower know when it's due back.

- **Get a library card:** If you don't already have a library card, go get one and use it. Librarians will help you find whatever kind of book you're looking for—funny, sad, scary—and even make some good suggestions if you tell them what kinds of books you like.

• **Animal careers:** Marty clearly loves animals. He even thinks he might be able to turn this love into a career. He thinks, "I want to be a vet someday," and "I could be a veterinarian's helper." How else could Marty—or you—turn a love for animals into a career? How about as a dog trainer, a groomer, an animal-control officer, a game warden, or a kennel owner, among other things? Choose one of these, or another animal-related career, then do some research to learn more about it. One good way to do this is to interview someone who is doing that job. Ask them what a typical day is like, what kind of training they had for their job, and what you can do at your age to help prepare you to do that kind of work in the future.

• **Cover to cover:** Design a new cover for *Shiloh*. Think about the cover's "job"—enticing a reader to pick up the book—as you decide which words and images you want to include in your design. When choosing what to illustrate, remember that the scenes that elicited the strongest response from you while reading the book will probably elicit a strong response in other readers. When you're done, compare your cover with the one on the book and think about which one works better, and why.

• **Bake a chocolate cake:** The day that Marty finishes his work to pay for Shiloh, his mother bakes a chocolate layer cake to celebrate. Here's a recipe for a chocolate layer cake you and an adult can make to celebrate something in your life—or simply to share the Prestons' joy at being able to call Shiloh their own.

Chocolate Celebration Cake

Cake Ingredients

2 cups flour

2 cups sugar

$3/4$ cup unsweetened cocoa

1 teaspoon baking soda

1 teaspoon baking powder

$1/2$ teaspoon salt

2 eggs

1 cup milk

$1/2$ cup vegetable oil

2 teaspoons vanilla

1 cup hot water

Icing Ingredients

1 stick ($1/2$ cup) butter or margarine

$2/3$ cup unsweetened cocoa

3 cups powdered sugar (or more, as needed)

5–6 tablespoons milk (or more, as needed)

1 teaspoon vanilla

Cake Directions

1. Preheat oven to 350°.
2. Grease and flour two 9-inch round pans.
3. Combine dry ingredients in a large bowl.
4. Add eggs, milk, oil, and vanilla. Mix well.
5. Stir in hot water.
6. Pour batter (which will be thin) into pans.
7. With an adult's help, put the pans into the preheated oven.
8. Bake for 30–35 minutes or until a toothpick inserted into the cake's middle comes out clean.
9. Cool completely before covering with chocolate icing.

Icing Directions

1. With an adult's help, melt the butter or margarine in a large pan.
2. Remove the pan from the heat and add the unsweetened cocoa. Combine well.
3. Alternately add powdered sugar and milk, mixing after each addition, for a smooth-spreading consistency. Add more sugar if the icing is too thin, more milk if it is too thick.
4. Stir in vanilla.
5. Spread on cooled chocolate cake.
6. Enjoy!

• **Go fly a kite:** When David Howard comes to visit Marty the day after Shiloh is attacked, he brings a kite that he plans to fly in Marty's meadow. Marty says the kite tail whipping in the breeze reminds him of how Shiloh's tail wags. Go fly a kite, and see if the tail reminds you of a dog's wagging tail. Before you go, however, remember the rules of safe kite-flying:

• Never fly kites in thunderstorms.
• Don't fly kites near power lines.
• Don't fly kites in places where someone may get hurt.
• Don't fly kites near airfields or roads.

• **Collect cans:** In *Shiloh*, Marty collects cans to make money. Collecting cans is a good way to recycle and make money. Check with a parent before going out to collect. You might even want to organize a can drive in your neighborhood or school, and see how many cans you can collect. Think about something worthwhile you can do with the money you raise. For example, you might want to donate it to your local humane society or another organization dedicated to helping abused animals. (You can research these organizations on the Internet or ask a local veterinarian for a recommendation.)

• **Winning ways:** Phyllis Reynolds Naylor won the 1992 Newbery Medal for *Shiloh*. Read one or two other Newbery-winning books and think about what it takes to be a winner. Some recent Newbery Medal–winning books are:

Crispin: The Cross of Lead by Avi (2003)
A Single Shard by Linda Sue Park (2002)

A Year Down Yonder by Richard Peck (2001)
Bud, Not Buddy by Christopher Paul Curtis (2000)
Holes by Louis Sachar (1999)
Out of the Dust by Karen Hesse (1998)
The View from Saturday by E. L. Konigsburg (1997)
The Midwife's Apprentice by Karen Cushman (1996)
Walk Two Moons by Sharon Creech (1995)
The Giver by Lois Lowry (1994)

- **So you'd like to own a...:** Marty quickly learns that there's more to owning a dog than loving it. Many people buy or adopt pets without thinking about the responsibilities of pet ownership and what is involved in pet care. Research a pet you have or would like to have. You can do this by getting books from the library about that pet, speaking with people who own that kind of pet, and interviewing veterinarians, animal-shelter workers, and pet-shop owners. Once you have collected all your information, make a brochure called "So You Want to Own a [Fill in the Pet]" that tells what it is like to own the pet and what care it needs. Include such things as equipment, food, exercise, veterinary care, and grooming. You might want to share your brochure with a veterinarian, animal-shelter worker, or pet-shop owner; if they like it, they can distribute copies to potential pet owners.

- **Earning what you want:** In the end, Marty had to pay Judd Travers forty dollars for Shiloh. Since he didn't have forty dollars, he worked for Judd for twenty hours at two dollars an hour to pay him. Is there something you really want but don't have the money to buy? Talk with a parent about ways in which you might be able to work to earn the money you need.

Related Reading

Other Shiloh Books by Phyllis Reynolds Naylor

Shiloh Season (1997)

Saving Shiloh (1997)

Other Books by Phyllis Reynolds Naylor

Beetles, Lightly Toasted (1987)

Bernie and the Bessledorf Ghost (1990)

The Fear Place (1994)

The Great Chicken Debacle (2001)

How I Came to Be a Writer (1978) (revised edition, 2001)

The Keeper (1986)

Maudie in the Middle (1988) (co-authored with her mother, Lura Schield Reynolds)

Night Cry (1984)

One of the Third-grade Thonkers (1988)

Walker's Crossing (1999)

Series by Phyllis Reynolds Naylor

The Club of Mysteries series (i.e., *The Grand Escape, The Healing of Texas Jake*)

The Alice series (i.e., *The Agony of Alice; Alice in Rapture, Sort Of*)

The Boys Versus the Girls series (i.e., *The Boys Start the War, The Girls Get Even*)

Dog Books—Fiction

Because of Winn-Dixie by Kate DiCamillo

Black Star, Bright Dawn by Scott O'Dell

The Call of the Wild by Jack London

A Dog Called Kitty by Bill Wallace

Lassie Come Home by Eric Knight

Love That Dog by Sharon Creech

Old Yeller by Fred Gipson

Sounder by William Howard Armstrong

Stone Fox by John Reynolds Gardiner

Where the Red Fern Grows by Wilson Rawls

White Fang by Jack London

Dog Books—Nonfiction

Beagle (Popular Dog Library) by Andrew Vallila

The Beagle (Learning About Dog series) by Charlotte Wilcox

The Complete Dog Book by American Kennel Club Staff

DK Pockets: Dogs by David Taylor

Dog by Juliet Clutton-Brock

Shelter Dogs: Amazing Stories of Adopted Strays by Pete Kehret

Understanding Man's Best Friend: Why Dogs Look and Act the Way they Do by Ann Squire

Other Children's Books That Take Place in West Virginia

Hound Heaven by Linda Oatman High

The Star Fisher and *Dream Soul* by Laurence Yep

Movies

Both *Shiloh* and *Shiloh 2: Shiloh Season* are available on VHS and DVD.

Bibliography

Books

Naylor, Phyllis Reynolds. *How I Came to Be a Writer.* New York: Simon & Schuster, 2001.

Naylor, Phyllis Reynolds. *Shiloh.* New York: Simon & Schuster, 1991.

Newspapers and magazines

The ALAN Review, Winter 1998, Volume 25, Number 2, p. 42.

Biography Today, 1993 Annual Cumulation, pp. 239–246.

The Columbus Dispatch, February 13, 1992, p. 18.

Horn Book Magazine, July 1992, Volume 68, Issue 4, pp. 404–415.

Journal of Youth Services in Libraries, Summer 1993, pp. 392–398.

The New York Times, May 10, 1992, p. 21.

School Library Journal, September 1991, p. 258.

Web sites

Educational Paperback Association:
   www.edupaperback.org/authorbios/Naylor_PhyllisReynolds.html

The Internet Public Library:
   www.ipl.org/youth/AskAuthor/Naylor.html

McCain Library and Archives, University Libraries, University of Southern Mississippi, deGrummond Collection:
   www.lib.usm.edu/~degrum/findaids/naylor.html

Phyllis Reynolds Naylor:
   www.simonsayskids.com/alice